# Oh, say did you know

Poems by

Ellen Hirning Schmidt

EVENING STREET PRESS
SACRAMENTO, CA

Evening Street Press

June, 2020

Sacramento, CA

**Winner, Helen Kay Chapbook Prize 2019**

Cover by Ellen Hirning Schmidt

ISBN: 978-1-937347-58-1

Printed in the United States of America

For Oskar

# Contents

Oh, say did you know


Oh say, did you know
that katharine lee bates wrote america the beautiful
while on a cross country train trip in 1893
By the dawn's early light i read about this 33 year old english teacher
and i began to think about
how every school child learns francis scott key wrote the star spangled banner
but here I am in my seventh decade and never heard of katharine lee bates
and i realized that the reason we have
a "bombs bursting in air" and "rocket's red glare" kind of song
instead of a "spacious skies" and "purple mountain majesties" kind of song is this:
how many women do you think were members of congress in 1931
when they voted on which kind of song we prefer?
And now which song we esteem
cleaves us wrong and right down the middle
splitting our fruited plains and alabaster cities
We watch and work and wait
at the twilight's last gleaming
for the man, not crowned with brotherhood, but peaked with an orange tiara
to crumble onto the amber waves of grain
and tumble into the shining sea.

The Harvest


What's going on,
I hear Marvin Gaye sing in my mind
No one can predict the future, a friend says to me,
In order to do good work, he continues,
you have to separate yourself from the outcome
I hear shots more often these days,
from just outside my neighborhood,
or perhaps closer than that
I can't quite tell which direction they come from
It's the cops practicing, my husband says
But they come from different directions, I say
I picked the first lettuce for lunch, he says
No one can predict the future
A hailstorm might come
smashing the garden bang-bang
It might come from some direction or all directions
squashing the flowered tranquility
The neighborhood's been quiet for a long time
The country's been restless during a few hundred years
But now like never before no one can predict the future
And we're down here in Whoville
while the Ludicrous Cartoon
in his gilt-lined, guilt-free tower,
reigns and reins and
rains down slashes into the gardens,
the fragile, tended, and wild, rugged gardens
What's going on
No one can predict the future
In order to keep a garden
you must imagine blossoms and fruits
but separate from the expectation of harvest
because no one can predict the future.

Playing Cards

He chooses the suits.
There's no seat for us at the table.
We're banished beyond the wall
For he is the Orange King
Off with our heads.

Winds are coming
outside and some
even inside,
flicking
The Joker
out of his very
small hands,
lifting it from his
very bad hand
till it lands atop the
house of cards and the
wall comes
tumbling down
while he
remains
in
the
tower
alone
in
his
shaft.

Rome, D.C.


Wily politicians and
unscrupulous swindlers
fleece the crowd of onlookers
while the Orange Emperor fiddles,
his hair reflected in the hellfires.
The crowd grows restless.
Some shout "Long Live" with balled fists.
Others frown, and
still more, ever more no longer remain silent.
As the naked emperor displays his fine doublet
and hose,
feet shift amid murmurs and grunts,
shovels appear and fists.
Someone shoves an elbow into a pickpocket's gut.
Screams and cries erupt from the crowd, no longer onlookers.
Smoke and flames reign.
Chaos rules now.
After 7 days and 7 nights,
ashes remain and a
bird flies up from the coals.
Painters and scribes recreate the flight.
Flutes and lyres imitate the song.
People emerge from their hiding places.
New emperors and pickpockets get born, but
poets, too, bear young, and those who
tend wounds of the fragile and sick also
go forth and multiply. In the
arid, hot marketplace,
still others carry baskets with their own
bright fruits.

# Citizens United

We all eat, though enjoy different foods.
We all drink water,
breathe air
We all smile, and though about different things, we make our
mouths spread across our faces and the
feeling of joy or amusement is known to us all.
We all cry with pain, even if not out loud, and with
loss, disappointment, with hurt feelings or anger.
Our teeth all chatter when we're cold.
We all sweat when too hot.
We all pee, we all poop, and nobody's smells like roses.
We all hope something good will happen.
We all have dreams by day or by night,
sometimes nightmares with fears and monsters.
We all know desire and longing.
We all want children to do well and be safe.
We all want to be healthy
We all.

# Good Fences

Mr. Said Ali, my neighbor, though I've changed his name a little,
lives in an expensive house I pass on my daily walks.
He hires laborers with skin much lighter than his
to build trellises, tend his garden, build a fence
around the house where he is seldom inside or outside.
When he moved in nine years ago
the only security system sign in the neighborhood
appeared in the grass in front of his house.
I made a map of the neighborhood -
who lives where, phone numbers, that sort of thing -
and put it and some garlic from our garden in his mailbox.
I don't know whether he received them.
Occasionally I see him outside and wave
and he waves back
and once I spoke hi and introduced myself.
 Ali, he said with a lived all his life in this country accent.
So I called Hello, Ali when I saw him
till I checked the tax maps and now say Mr. Ali.
Once he asked me, how do I know when these apples are ready?
I told him about shaking the tree and windfalls.
Later on that fall he said he'd keep his 100 lb sack of apples on his back porch.
What kept me from mentioning mice, deer, freezing and thawing, decay?
When there's a neighborhood gathering he never comes,
Neighbors don't know his name.
No one has any idea who he is, his email or phone number,
but everyone seems to practice peaceful coexistence.
I pass his house on my walks
and I wonder and wonder
who decides about staying inside
and who decides about remaining outside
invisible fences.

Geese

Canada geese, hundreds of them,
black and white lumps
strewn across the field as I drive past, they're
sitting, waddling, lying down, chatting, squawking, shitting.
An hour later when I return, they're gone.
What did they decide?
How did they decide?
Where to next?
What was important?
Could we manage our affairs with the same messy peace?

Standing with her legs apart

Standing with her legs apart,
like Marilyn Monroe over the subway heating vent
her creamy calf-length chiffon skirt
flows and billows like a jellyfish in the ocean
she feels the breeze blow across her skin, her long bare legs
(If you are one of her grown children reading this
you might already regret it)
As she wakes up,
erotic steam and   wonder stir in her,
even at the age      of 69, a racy number which
her generation       thought they invented.
If you are a          grown child
of anyone,             then you know
because                 she is a child of someone too, that we
always                   sought to keep that trusted territory safe
(if we                    were lucky and certainly wished to if we weren't), the
guarded                 land only we and our parents inhabited together
where                    sheltered from the muggings of a steroid sexed world
trusting                  that land, believing, later
wishing,                 and pretending to ourselves that our
parents                  never had a single sexual thought or dream, or
godforbid               act, except
maybe the              one that
determined             our very existence.

# Memory Foam

On the shore
day and night meet for momentary counsel.
Here dreams recently roiled in dark oceans become foam,
resting for a breath on the beach,
revealing in light what transpired in the fathomless night.
Waiting winds pull some sticky bubbles away from others
flicking them in the air
returning them to the yawning sea,
tide taking the remaining bits.
Shore and sea meet for
fleeting exchange in a
moment of awareness and
inform one another of their creative work.
Then day and night
wake and dream,
sea and shore
return to sculpt the same tales again and again
without regard to age, time, place, or scape
They know so little of each other and
they know everything about each other,
each in each,
their quick embrace leaves no trace.

I have so many thoughts


I have so many, many, many thoughts
Morning, noon, and in the night.
I keep paper and pen everywhere:  car, purse, toilet tank, bedside table
But I rarely capture 1/100,000,000 of them
Capture.  A funny expression,
how tyrannical to hastily grab a thought or feeling,
then codify it into impossibly confining symbols.
Yet how else to keep it safe?
Safe?  Safe on paper, in ink?
Perhaps more secure floating
waiting in the
ether
ready to enter another sleeping or wakeful being
who will capture it.
Or will it slip away,
weightless,
blowing on
beyond
a wisp of milkweed.

Lines Written in Low Light

This morning cold and soft,
just before I woke, the
walls stood around me
but the sky, the blue black
sky rose above me,
open
inviting, where the
stars sing and glisten
gleaming in place, in time with some ancient,
strange and silent music, and
perched on invisible branches
roosting through the long and dangling winter sky
giving breath to a far off planet's spring as we here
restless in our own sky
try to undo our yesterdays
while considering our tomorrows.
Now in softer blue light
I sit warmed in five layers and a hat,
tea before and in me, the
woodpecker has flown from her
spangled perch in the
dawn's early light to
carve a sculpture in the
dead tree that is home.
The music from the stars that
crept in last night and blew the
sweeping pageant of stars, now
falls at my feet in crumbs
as the bird flies off.

## This morning snaps

This morning snaps with cold
sunlight over the neighbor's pond and trees
Outside my window the shadows sit still on the snow
under the bird feeder.
If you think this is going to be one of those nature poems
you might want to skip the next few lines
where I will write
how I wake in the night to my
brain's requiem chant
descending into pits of Dread of all
Dante's levels Trump-etted this year, and
Dread of a fall onto the hard ground or a
Fall from the Grace of our lives, or
Disease.
Don't resume reading just yet,
I'll let you know when.
Where was I?
Ah yes, Dis-ease
Dread, Debility, Doom
watching as beloveds falter,
one's own body disintegrates.
No one escapes, you know.
I used to half believe before I gave birth, that
my baby might be an exception, wouldn't need diapers.
But we don't escape diapers on our bottoms, at the
bottom and upper ends of our lives often too.
All these thoughts circled my wagon last night.
You can read the next few lines if you like, about the
top spikes of the tall pines
bright in the bluing with the
light and promise of day,
cold, yes, but manageable in the
light,
warmth of tea,
wrap of gentle wool and fleece, the
softness of our time together
this morning.

Getting to it

Though getting on
I'm still getting around
Managing to get by
Getting up each morning
Got past rough spots
And now –
Well, I am finally getting on it
Getting down in the music.

When we talk

I am there
with you
when we talk
whoever you might be
as if there is
nothing
more important
than to
be here now
together
And there isn't.

## Snow and Roses

"Where are the snows of yesteryear?"
my father asks no one in particular
his big hand over my little one as we
stroll past seaside cottages swaddled in scrabbly rose blooms
And even at five, I know what he means.
Now I look at roses,
impossibly garish ones planted in front of public buildings,
or the swoon-filled lust-petaled blossoms
lazing gracefully on big unruly bushes
I push my nose in one and breathe, eyes closed
As June weeks move on, petals drop one by one
Fall in a thin ruby carpet,
first lustrous, then brown, curled, and damp
And I think of snows and roses and my father
all so here, all so gone.

# Taking Wing

We brought her in last night from the
cool days and cooler nights
(yet still remarkably without frost)
stuck in her chrysalis birth canal
two orange painted wings mostly emerged
head and body still partially in the shell
Is she moving, we ask each other
Yes, yes ! Wings – her wings move
Yes, and the beginning of appendages move on their own or
maybe like a frog's legs, my husband says,
long after death still moving with electric current
warmed by the living breath from our mouths?
Placing a piece of warm cooked apple
near her on the plate left from the all afternoon applesauce making
Will she come to it? Will she come to?
I check the plate before bed yet another time
This morning I expected – well, half expected,
well, hoped anyway I'd
see her flying around the kitchen but
now it's clear
She'd struggled enough and
like all of us, sooner or later in
whatever stage,
conformed to those strictly enforced laws of
life and death
I look at the lifeless butterfly wings on the plate and
remember many years ago when my toddler
brought me a post-life papery moth
Aware of this early lesson in her life
I explain that the moth is no longer alive, is 'dead'
She looks at me, frowns, then brightens and says,
'Nona make it more dead',
then with her small palms
she brushes back and forth over the moth
whose powdery wings
fly like dust.

## When I looked out my window

When I looked out my window as a child,
I could see the branches of the maples
make letters of the alphabet
where they crossed each other.
K's and X's were popular,
especially in winter when
leaves were gone and
wind whisked and whipped
big branches and smaller ones.
Now I see only intersecting lines
angles, shapes, spaces
framed by green or orange leaves or in the
carpet on the floor, faces of a
dog racing ahead or a
monkey with hollow eyes.

Has it not been always so?


Now is the time
when nights surge long
abridging the days
Our days are darkened, still darkening
while our nights, bleached by electronic pallor
radiate divisiveness among us.
At night railings and fences cast full
shadows on the snow from the high noon moon.
Only the deep wee hours, which they say are
darkest before the dawn,
provide almost silent saturated black for
buried seeds to germinate.
In these oases of kindness
reason's tender shoots can
burst forth unseen.
Throughout the ages,
has it not been always so?

I already learned to stand on my head

At ten, I wanted to be the first person to
go to the moon,
discover a cure for cancer, the
first woman president.
Years later I thought,
before I die, I'll
learn to stand on my head,
learn  to speak Spanish,
eat as much chocolate ice cream with
chocolate chips in a sugar cone as fits and a
scone and a popover.
Now,
before I die
we'll share another funny story of a neighbor and a
crazy dream in the morning, I'll
write poems and paint and draw and glue,
share them with you,
feel energy
thrumming through my veins and
share that with you, too.
Before I die I'll
read wonderful books that pull me into them
We'll eat homemade pizza and
your pesto with our basil and
one of every vegetable in your garden.
Before I die I will do all the things that I
do each day,
live just as today,
this day,
all days.
No need to go anywhere or to
do anything special -
It's already as special as it can get.

The summer's flanked by gold

Summer's flanked by gold, my father told me.
Forsythia blooms burst into spires leading the parade,
soon tender pastels appear
followed all the short summer long by
fireworks rioting with saturated colors.
But wait, out on my walk this mid July day, way too soon, the
first fingers of goldenrod protrude from their stalks
Now?  Not today with
school still weeks and weeks away?
My father would point them out to me at the
end of August, the goldenrod spears bordered by
deeply dyed greens portending
fall's circus of color and
halting glorious freedom for a
long, long while ahead and
sadness creeps into my long ago new school shoes,
tightens around my all summer long bare feet as
I gazed out of the classroom window into the frame of
sunshine where I am not.

# Treatise

"Probably 80 years old," he says,
"It's usually the people who see them
every day who notice the changes."
We're standing near the tree's fresh corpse,
3 rope-wielding men it's taken to bring her to the ground.
I'd seen the long thin crack in her trunk as we ate our
last outdoor lunch of the season
sitting below her and looking up into her crown 80 feet above our yard,
"Yeah, they begin to decay inside. No rush, but it should come down,
best before the winter winds,
being that close to your house and all," he had said.
We hadn't slept the night before for love of her, living side by side with us for three decades,
spangled full-leafed branches in summer's green above the picnics, then
red, orange, yellow later on arcing over us,
falling into crisp elegant carpets, huge rusty, rustling collar around her base, then during the
long white winter this year her felled body lay on the ground stiff and silent,
limbs in frozen atrophy,
her flat base spanning 37 inches.
Later on in the first warm days, clear bleeding sap
weeps from her even stump, and
summons all manner of
insects and a few butterflies
drunk in bliss, skimming the surface of her pooled juice.
Below, sprouting in a tender green ring
around her ample stump,
nursling baby maples
now grow in profusion.

# What she said

Just after he died I whispered into his ear,
my mother told me afterward,
And then, when the doctor came in, she asked him
What should I do now?
Well, you have to carry on somehow, he told her
But that is not what I meant, she told me
She meant what are the to-do's after someone dies,
in this case my father,
(Because she knew she would be able to handle the rest)
Now eighteen years after her death
and thirty-five after his,
I am wondering what she whispered.

# Step Right Up and Try Your Luck

Just one bolt of lightning
fried the answering machine, as it had
two weeks earlier.
What are the chances?
It took only one train to kill my sister.
Strange hand, finger on an unknown trigger,
cocked without aim in
absurd Russian Roulette.
Somehow,
sometime
one shoe or another will drop,
climatic catastrophe or
dread disease
might claim victory.
Of course there's a chance that an
errant comet will
take care of all of us at once.
Last night the wind formed
archipelagoes of slippery pine needles with
dry oak leaves into gliding mines on the road.
This morning, picking my way in the
channels between them in
another game of
chance, I am
armed to the teeth
with Hope.

Tears from the Book of Questions

"Do tears not spilled
wait in small lakes?"*
Where do they come from
before they reach the lakes?
Do they come from larger lakes or
smaller lakes?
Do they cascade over precipices
making waterfalls
salty as the ocean,
salty as our blood?
Do tears well up from the earth like
bubbling artesian springs
giving life
cleansing old wounds
(however painful from the salt)?
Are tears the same tears from a water cycle of drying and
spilling and drying again?

Are your tears my tears?
Are everyone's tears everyone's tears?
Do our tears form deep caverns in the
recesses of the creviced aorta?
Do they drop one by one from the
membrane ceiling of the
fleshy floor in the
dark tunnels of the heart
forming stalactites and stalagmites,
imprisoned forever in the locked chambers?

What is the speed of tears?
Do they rampage, clatter,
spatter, scatter in the wind?
Does one ooze, agonizingly waiting for
brother or sister to jump first,
leading a snail's trail one by one from
the tender spot?
When they pool,
do tears unite in
joy or sadness, bewilderment or pain or
just into a silent puddle?

Can you tell time by a tear?
Gauge the appearance of each one on a blade of morning grass?
Watch each one fall through the cinched waist of an hourglass?
Hear each one plop at regular intervals into a
pot of tear water tea?
Smell each tear turn to ice, then
melt, flow, and turn to ice again?

Can the path of a tear tell a story if
you follow its trail, first
wet, then invisible salty ink that
only your tongue can decipher?

Can a tear quench my thirst or yours?
Can a lake of tears quench the thirst of thousands?
Or simply parch their throats?

If I hurled my tears into space
would they come back at me at the
speed of sound or light, like
spitting out the open window of a fast car?
Or would they fly to Venus and sizzle and sear?
Or to Mars and evaporate?

Where does a tear go when it rains?
Does it put on galoshes and carry an
umbrella to protect its perfect shape?
Is the perfect shape of a tear, once created,
bound for destruction?
What is the equation for the creation of a tear?
What is the formula for its destruction?

Do tears have questions?
Maybe.


*The first two lines of this poem are from *The Book of Questions* by Pablo Neruda

Rhino, you whisper


"Rhino," you whisper
to the others in the dream.
They look in the direction you are pointing.
"Get down," someone says, "on the ground."
You all lie still in the green wind-combed grass,
here at the edge of a cliff,
precariously high
above the red rock mountains and
sandstone canyons way below.
You lie together in a huddle, silent,
conserving breath to avoid his notice.
You sense his quiet nearness and
feel the billows of his warm breath,
almost sweet even, on your
neck, shoulder, arm as you
picture the weight of his grim scythe.
Is this your last
exquisite moment on earth
before he gores you?
Or, and so it turns out,
he is leaving you behind,
with puffed humid breaths moving on,
hot and close enough to prickle your skin.
As his hind quarters lumber past,
you imagine his sharp sickle
slivering the edge of the cliff and
you think
you will have
at least
this day,

The seas run high


Send an S-O-S?
Or just arrange the deck chairs?
All end up fish food

Send up flares once more?
Strike the band up yet again?
Both, one, or neither?

The seas do run high
What to do to stay afloat?
You write this last line.

Once

Once I sat with a group of women all writing about *once*
Once they started to write, there was no stopping some
Once one paused, removed and replaced the cap of her pen
Once two left hands squiggled across their papers, nine right hands wiggled the other direction
Once one of the women raised her head, looked deeply into the ceiling light with eyes closed
Once five right legs crossed over left and two left crossed over right, four feet flat on the floor
Once the minds of the women began to run freely, their thoughts traveled past farmhouses, up
long staircases, through meadows of wild poppies, into deep woods where thrushes sing
Once they began to think about *once,* there was no end because they saw their reflections in
antique glass, heard soft singing far away and mysterious, remembering things once said to them
Once one heard words that burned and seared the flesh in her brain and left a sad scar
Once one woman believed a thought that she found later to no longer be true
Once a girl tried on a pair of shiny red shoes with buckles, looked in the mirror down at her feet
Once she opened her umbrella as the sky burst and saturated her, leaving rivulets on her skin
Once a woman here found a pimple on her nose and pushed it till it burst onto the mirror
Once, some time later, she pulled the first white hair out of the strand at her temple
Once a woman fell in love and into bed, then laughed and smoked a cigarette
Once she called across the creeping night for a child still at large playing
Once a woman swam naked loving the ripples that traveled like handwriting away from her body
Once a woman read a poem, years later silently moving her lips to its words driving her car
Once a woman caught a small chipmunk the cat had caught and released it into a bush
Once she stirred soup, danced a jig to music on the radio, not really a jig, but it didn't matter.
Once a woman stabbed her finger with a needle and it bled onto her blue checkered pocket
Once a woman wrote on a piece of paper, then tore it up, then wished she hadn't
Once a woman cried, sobbing and wiping snot on her sleeve
Once a long day behind her, a woman sighed as she pulled one shoe off with the toe of the other
Once a woman held a fragile woman's hand, faint electric squeeze before the life current ceased
Once it was morning, then it was night.
Once it was dark and then it was light.
Once she was born

Twice she gave birth
Thrice she ate today
Four seasons she knew last year
Five fingers she sees on each hand
Six times she swallowed
Seven times she reconsidered then did it anyway
Eight times she pushed the button through the hole
Nine times she called and got a busy signal
Ten times she tried to thread a needle
Eleven times she wondered which way to go
Twelve times she returned to the same spot
A hundred times she opened her mouth to speak
A thousand times she took a deep breath
A million times she's been thankful to be alive.

The Cave of Forgotten Dreams

*-Chauvet, France-*

Did they cry out in the night, and by
day inscribe wooly mammoths,
cave bears, rhinos, lions, and
horses, yes, whinnying horses running,
neighing through their moist nostrils in the cave,
shaded in the darkening of time,
engraved in shadows on the walls.

Your eye catches flickers of forms
shut away, unseen, closed off from
star and sun for thirty thousand years.

Hard crystals cover charcoal
figures drawn on curved walls by hands like yours.
Reach out and you could touch a
horse galloping or the artist's handprint.
Drippings frozen in glistening smooth stone
meet others below.
Notice the sacred cave bear skull placed just so.

Inhale migrations of breath, the whiff of
lives of two and four and six legs,
humid smells of dried blood and bone cells,
powdered insect wings,
hair fragments ground into the
floor of the cave.
What small insects, rodents or worms
breathed the air that the
painter inhaled and exhaled as he drew?
How many inhalations, and exhalations through
era after era outside the cave while
inside the cave none at all?

Deep inside the cave
bison and human woman
unite in erotic embrace on protruding stone and
spirits spring inside the night of her body's cavern in a world where
animals and humans blur into one another's realms.

Silence

Darkness

Listen in the labyrinth to the
acoustics of heart beats – yours and theirs -
sounds of hairy humans telling
unknown stories heard by
no one for thirty thousand years.
You listen, your brain alight in its own
labyrinth of worlds within worlds, in its own
dark universe.
The passageways of your brain, of their brains
close and open in rhythm,
revealing a moment, a
glimmer of recognition.

Your brain asleep,
now awakens in the
cave of forgotten dreams.


A nod to Werner Herzog's same-titled film.

Star Bright
*for all the children*

twinkle, twinkle
how I marvel that
we gleam like diamonds and
just for a moment
touch each other.
up above the world so high,
along our milky ways, I,
leaning on my star, and you Pegasus,
galloping
across the universe, in the
changing sky,
how I wonder.

# Acknowledgements

I am immensely grateful to Evening Street Press and Editor Barbara Bergman for selecting my work for the Helen Kay Chapbook Prize.

My gratitude to editors Mary Azrael and Kendra Kopelke for choosing my poem *Oh, say did you know* for the Passager Poetry Contest Issue, which helped set me on my way. My appreciation extends to Charles Portolano, editor of The Avocet, for bringing me into a supportive community of poets and for publishing *Taking Wing, Treatise, Geese, Memory Foam,* and *The seas run high,* and to Glenn Lyvers, editor of Poetry Quarterly, for publishing *Snow and Roses*, *Step Right Up and Try Your Luck, The summer's flanked by gold,* and *Rome, D.C.* Thanks go as well to Caesura, for publishing *I already learned to stand on my head.*

Kathleen Hunter's self-titled 'Medici' enthusiasm and support came at the right moment to shift my feelings toward sharing my poems publicly. Nora Blanck encouraged me years ago to share my work although I was not ready yet. Tony Difabbio, Marian Difabbio, Carol Dubiel, Shirley Hogg, Candace Mingins and Steve Weed each gave me initial encouragement to believe in my work. Joel Savishinsky's solid confidence in my poetry boosted my own confidence in it. I am grateful to Barbara Lydecker Crane who took time to read this ms with extra care. Generous gratitude to Mary Azrael for her wholehearted embrace of my poems.

Thank you to my mentor, the late Louise Albert, who taught me how to read when I was a child and decades later how to write. And to my students, thank you! We are all each other's teachers.

Appreciation goes to my daughter Nora for her focused, positive, endorsements, and to my son Robin for his much valued tech support.
For his kindness, patience, and ever much more, I am thankful beyond a poet's words to my husband Oskar.